Contents

INTRODUCTION

IN FLIGHT

FUN & GAMES

HEY PRESTO!

ON THE WATER

ACTION PACKED

SNAP, SNAP!

Introduction

Origami has been popular in Japan for hundreds of years and is now loved all around the world. Action origami is a special kind of origami that can be made to move or perform some sort of action. From a floating motorboat to a flying helicopter, and an egg-laying hen to a barking dog, this book is packed with fantastic models that can fly, float, snap, spin, jump, and even perform magical illusions. All you need to get started is a square of paper, your fingers, and some nifty folds!

ACTION ORIGAMI

PAPER MODELS THAT FLOAT, FLY, SNAP, AND SPIN!

ARCTURUS

This edition published in 2016 by Arcturus Publishing Limited
26/27 Bickels Yard, 151–153 Bermondsey Street,
London SE1 3HA

Models and photography by Belinda Webster and Michael Wiles
Written by Joe Fullman
Designed by Tokiko Morishima
Edited by Frances Evans

ISBN: 978-1-78599-005-2
CH004842NT
Supplier 26, Date 1215, Print run 4492

Printed in China

Getting Started

The paper used in origami is thin but strong, so that it can be folded many times. You can use ordinary scrap paper, as long as it's not too thick.

A lot of the origami models in this book are made with the same folds. This introduction explains some of the ones that will appear most, so it's a good idea to master these folds before you start. When making the projects, follow the key below to find out what the lines and arrows mean. And always crease well!

KEY

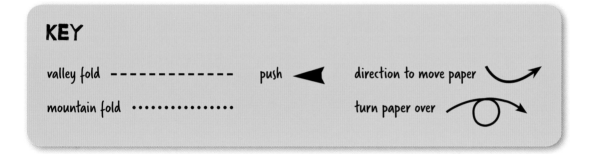

valley fold - - - - - - - - - - - - - - -   push ◄   direction to move paper ⤷

mountain fold ⋅⋅⋅⋅⋅⋅⋅⋅⋅⋅⋅⋅⋅⋅⋅⋅⋅⋅⋅   turn paper over ↻

MOUNTAIN FOLD

To make a mountain fold, fold the paper so that the crease is pointing up toward you, like a mountain.

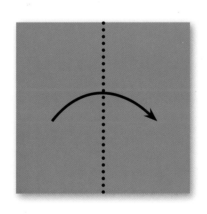
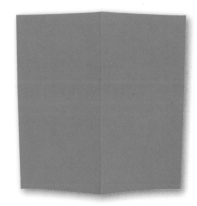

VALLEY FOLD

To make a valley fold, fold the paper the other way, so that the crease is pointing away from you, like a valley.

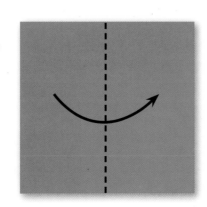
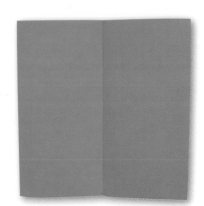

INSIDE REVERSE FOLD

This is useful if you want to flatten part of an origami model. It will come in handy for your Magician's Rabbit (page 50) and Jumping Horse (page 76).

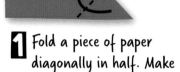 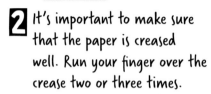

1 Fold a piece of paper diagonally in half. Make a valley fold on one point and crease.

2 It's important to make sure that the paper is creased well. Run your finger over the crease two or three times.

3 Unfold and open up the corner slightly. Refold the crease nearest to you into a mountain fold.

Open

 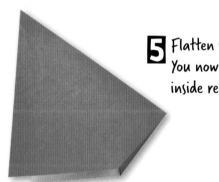

4 Open up the paper a little more and then tuck the tip of the point inside. Close the paper. This is the view from the underside of the paper.

5 Flatten the paper. You now have an inside reverse fold.

OUTSIDE REVERSE FOLD

This is great if you want to make part of your model stick out. You'll need it for the Duckling (page 60) and Barking Dog (page 90).

1 Fold a piece of paper diagonally in half. Make a valley fold on one point and crease.

2 It's important to make sure that the paper is creased well. Run your finger over the crease two or three times.

3 Unfold and open up the corner slightly. Refold the crease farthest away from you into a mountain fold.

Open

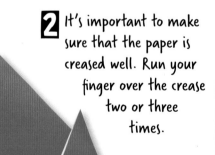 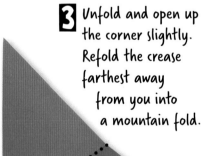

4 Open up the paper a little more and start to turn the corner inside out. Then close the paper when the fold begins to turn.

5 You now have an outside reverse fold. You can either flatten the paper or leave it rounded out.

In Flight

It's a bird... it's a plane... it's flying origami!
Take to the skies with this great collection of
flapping and flying models.

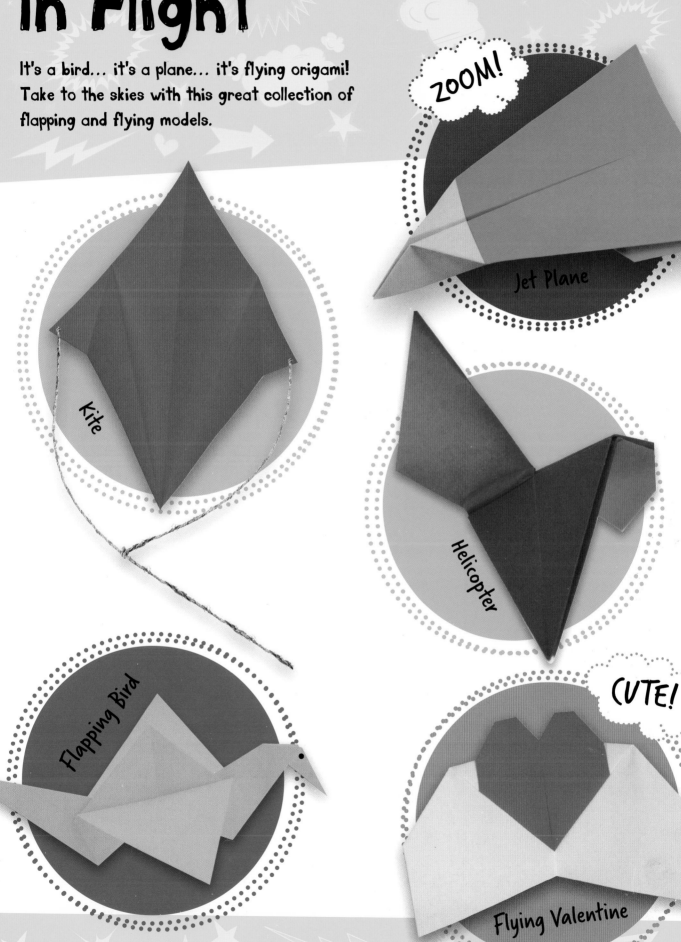

ZOOM!

Jet Plane

Kite

Helicopter

Flapping Bird

CUTE!

Flying Valentine

Kite

Up, up, and away! This crazy kite really does fly. Just be sure to attach some string so that it doesn't blow away.

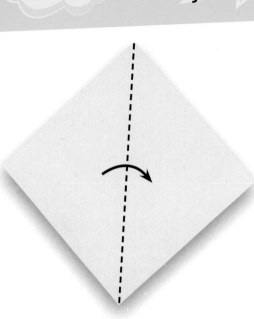

1 Valley fold the paper in half from left to right, forming a triangle.

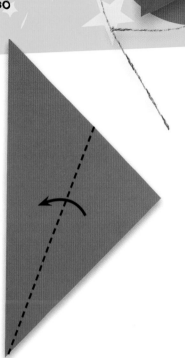

2 Take the right-hand corner of the top layer of paper and fold it back to the central crease.

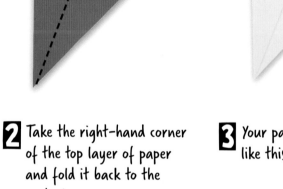

3 Your paper should now look like this.

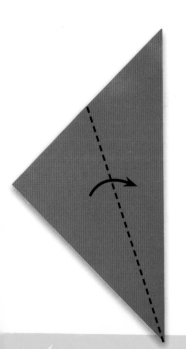

4 Turn the paper over from left to right, then fold the left-hand corner over to the right edge.

5 Fold the top edge of the white paper down, so it lines up with the left-hand edge.

6 Turn the paper over from right to left.

7 Fold the top edge of the white paper over so it lines up with the right-hand edge.

8 Your paper should look like this.

10 Make two holes at the tips and attach some string to your kite. Head out on a windy day and see how high it can soar!

9 Carefully pull the folds out so the paper can stand upright.

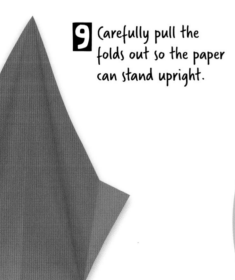

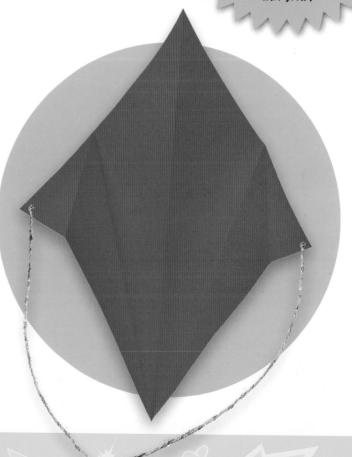

Flapping Bird

This classic origami crane has a hidden twist...
it can flap! Follow these instructions to fold your
own flapping bird.

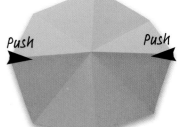

1 Valley fold your paper
diagonally both ways,
then unfold.

2 Valley fold along the
horizontal and vertical
lines. Unfold and turn
your paper over.

3 Push the left- and right-
hand corners together,
so the shape starts to
collapse.

Push　　　*Push*

Press

4 Your model should now look
like this. Press down the top
to create a square.

5 Valley fold the top right-
hand layer to meet the
central crease.

6 Do the same on the left.
Then turn your model over
and repeat steps 5 and 6
on the other side.

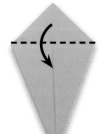

7 Valley fold the
top flap down.

8 Unfold the creases you made at
steps 5, 6, and 7.

Flatten　　　*Flatten*

9 Gently lift the
bottom flap upward
to make a pocket.
Flatten the edges.

10 Your model should now look like this.

11 Turn your model over. Repeat steps 9 and 10 on the other side.

12 Valley fold, then mountain fold, the right-hand point.

13 Now, turn this into an inside reverse fold (page 6). This is your bird's tail.

15 Valley fold the left-hand tip as shown, then make another inside reverse fold. This is your bird's head.

16 Valley fold the wing. Turn over and repeat to form the second wing.

14 Valley fold, then mountain fold, the left-hand point. Turn this into an inside reverse fold, too.

17
To make the wings move, hold your bird's neck and pull firmly on its tail. Your origami bird is ready to leave the nest!

Jet Plane

This sleek, streamlined plane is built for speed. Follow the instructions carefully to make sure it flies as fast as possible!

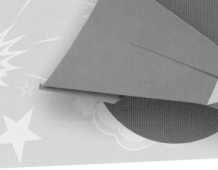

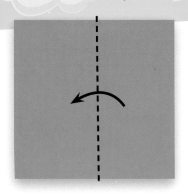

1 Place your paper like this. Valley fold it from right to left, then unfold.

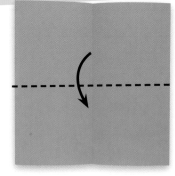

2 Valley fold the paper from top to bottom, then unfold.

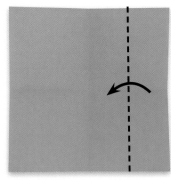

3 Valley fold the right-hand edge to meet the vertical crease.

4 Turn your paper over from top to bottom, so the fold you made in step 3 stays on the right-hand side.

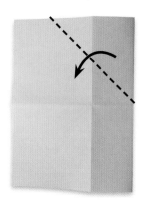

5 Valley fold the top right-hand corner so it lines up with the horizontal crease.

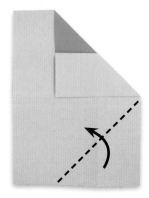

6 Valley fold the bottom right-hand corner so it lines up with the horizontal crease.

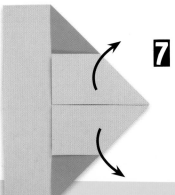

7 Unfold the folds you made in steps 5 and 6.

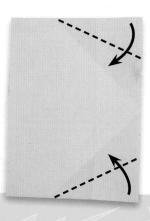

8 Make two new valley folds with the right-hand corners, so they line up with the creases you made in steps 5 and 6.

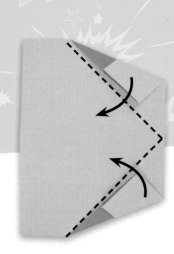

9 Fold the right-hand corners over again so that they line up with the crease in the middle. This is the nose of the jet.

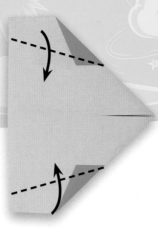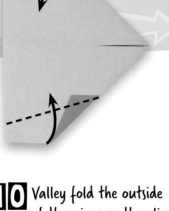

10 Valley fold the outside of the wings so they line up with the edges of the nose section.

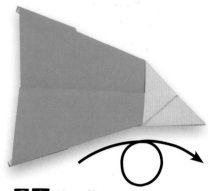

11 Valley fold the rear of the wings so they line up with the outside edges.

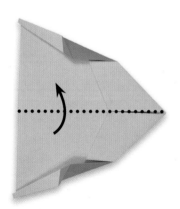

12 Mountain fold the paper in half along the central crease.

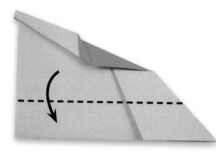

13 Valley fold the top wing down, as shown.

14 Turn the paper over.

15 Repeat step 13 on the other side and your model is nearly complete.

16 Unfold the wings, even them up, and your plane is ready to take to the skies.

Flying Valentine

Make it a Valentine's Day to remember by creating this cute flying heart card. Then send it over to that special someone... without them knowing, of course!

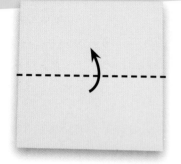

1 Position the paper like this, white side up. Valley fold the paper in half but don't crease it.

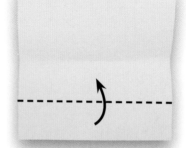

2 Just pinch the middle to show where the halfway point is. Then valley fold the bottom half of the paper to the middle point and crease.

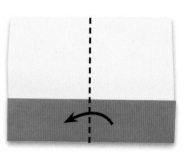

3 Fold the paper in half from right to left, but again don't crease.

4 Gently pinch the paper at the bottom to show where the middle point is. Turn the paper over from left to right.

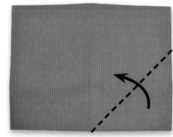

5 Fold the bottom right corner to the middle, using the pinch mark as a guide.

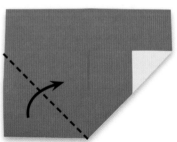

6 Fold the bottom left corner to the middle, again using the pinch mark as a guide.

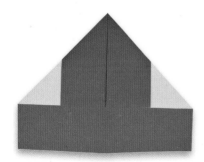

7 Rotate your paper so the pointed end is facing away from you, then turn it over from right to left.

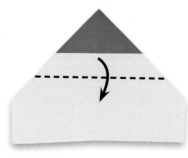

8 Valley fold the top point so it's about 2 cm (3/4 inch) from the bottom edge.

9 Your paper should look like this. Turn it over from left to right.

14

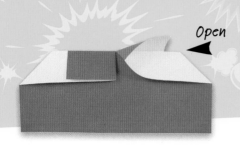

Open

Open

10 Use your finger to open up the flap in the top right corner to form a pocket.

11 Flatten the pocket to form a triangular shape, like this.

12 Now, use your finger to open up the flap in the top left corner to form a pocket.

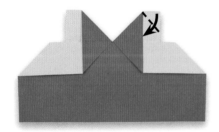

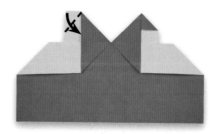

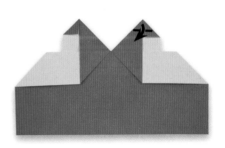

13 Flatten the pocket to form a triangular shape. Then make a small diagonal fold in the top right corner.

14 Make a small diagonal fold in the top left corner.

15 Fold over the top right point.

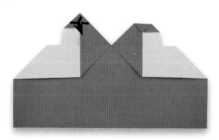

16 Fold over the top left point.

18
Turn your paper over and open the card up. Your heart is ready to fly to your Valentine!

17 Your paper should now look like this. Mountain fold it down the middle.

15

Helicopter

You may get dizzy watching this amazing spinning helicopter whirling around. The higher you drop it, the more it will spin!

1 Place the paper like this.

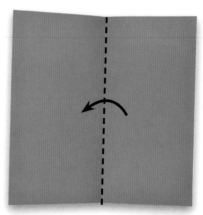

2 Valley fold it in half from right to left, then unfold.

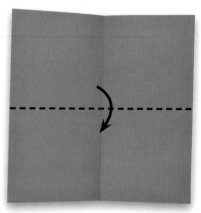

3 Now valley fold the paper in half from top to bottom, then unfold.

4 Turn the paper over. Then valley fold it in half diagonally from right to left.

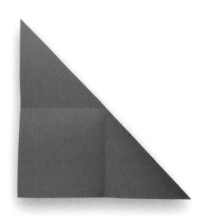

5 Your paper should look like this.

6 Unfold the paper and turn it so the diagonal fold made in step 4 is now horizontal.

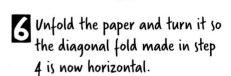

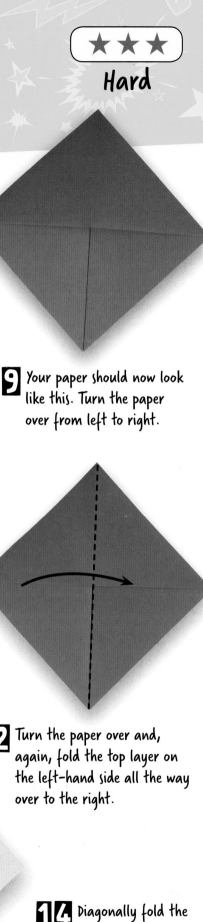

7 Push the sides together so the paper starts to fold up.

8 The paper should fold itself into a square. With the open side facing you, valley fold the top layer of the paper in half.

9 Your paper should now look like this. Turn the paper over from left to right.

10 Again, valley fold the top layer of paper in half.

11 Then fold the top layer on the left-hand side all the way to the right, so that the top layer is all white.

12 Turn the paper over and, again, fold the top layer on the left-hand side all the way over to the right.

13 Diagonally fold the top left layer to the middle line.

14 Diagonally fold the top right layer to the middle line.

Helicopter... continued

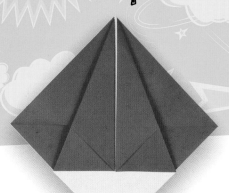

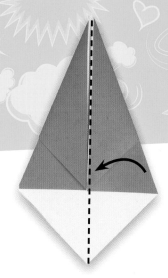

15 Your paper should look like this. Turn it over.

16 Fold the left-hand side to the middle line, like this. Then fold the right-hand side to the middle line, too.

17 Fold the top right-hand layer over to the left so there's no more white showing.

19 There should now be a clear gap in the bottom half of the paper. Valley fold the right flap up to the top.

20 Mountain fold the left-hand flap the other way.

18 Turn the paper over. Again, fold the top right-hand layer over to the left so there's no more white showing.

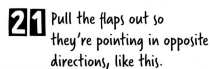

21 Pull the flaps out so they're pointing in opposite directions, like this.

22

Hold the helicopter with the two flaps at the top, gently release it, and watch it spin.

18

Fun and Games

In this chapter you can learn to fold some fantastic origami games and toys, from a set of dominoes to a super spinning top.

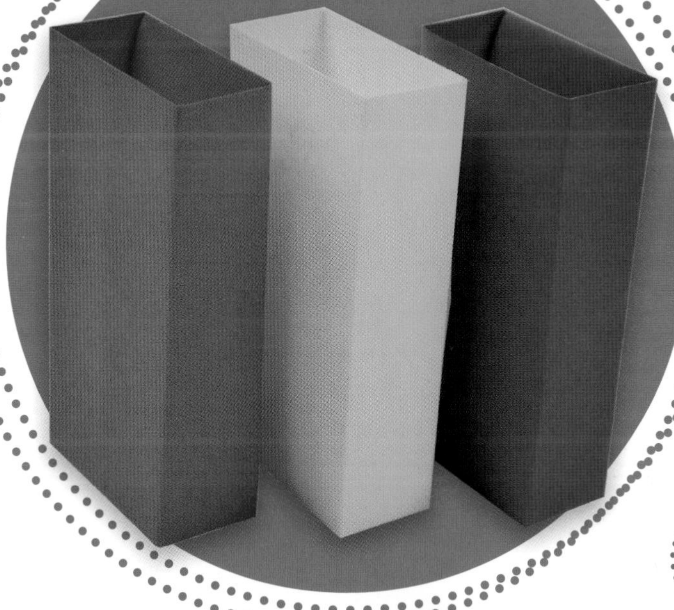

Dominoes

Basketball Hoop

SLAM DUNK!

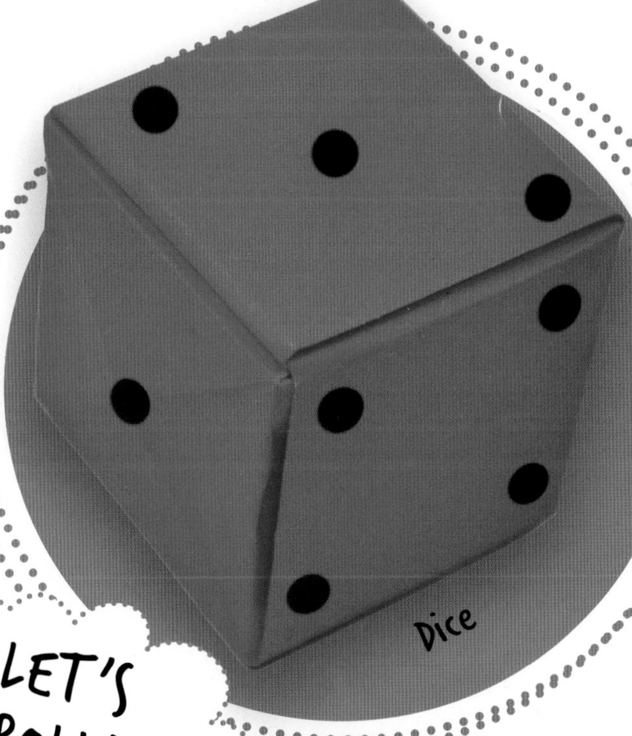

Dice

LET'S ROLL!

Spinning Top

Dominoes

It's great fun to send a row of dominoes toppling over. Follow these instructions to make a few, carefully line them up, and watch them fall!

1 Place the paper like this. Valley fold the bottom edge up to the top, but don't crease the line.

2 Just make a small crease on the left edge, then unfold the paper.

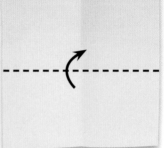

3 Turn it 90° to the right, so the small crease is at the top. Valley fold the bottom edge up to the top, but again don't crease the line.

4 Again, make a small crease on the left edge.

5 Unfold and then valley fold the bottom edge to the middle (marked by the small crease).

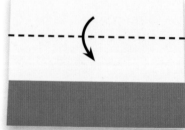

6 This time make a hard crease all the way along the fold. Then fold the top half down to the middle, too.

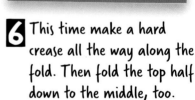

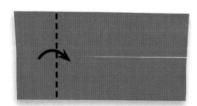

7 There should be slightly more white showing on the right than on the left. Fold the left edge to the crease mark in the middle.

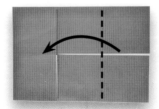

8 Fold the right edge all the way to the left edge.

9 Your paper should look this. Unfold the right flap.

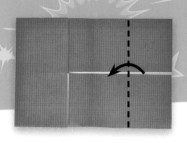

10 Fold the right edge over so it meets the edge of the left flap.

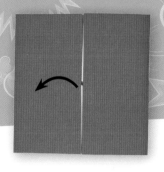

11 Your paper should now look like this. Unfold the left flap.

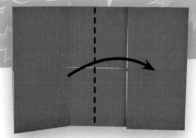

12 Fold the left edge all the way to the right edge.

13 Your paper should look like this, with a vertical crease about a quarter of the way from the left edge, and a small horizontal crease on the right edge.

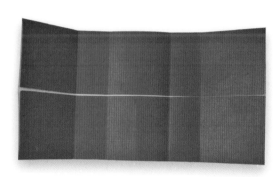

14 Completely unfold the two flaps, so your paper looks like this.

Push

15 Curl the paper over and insert the left flap (the one with the crease mark) inside the right-hand flap (the one without a crease mark).

18 Make a set of dominoes using different paper!

Push

16 Keep pushing the left flap inside the other flap.

17 Once it's all the way inside, your domino is ready.

Basketball Hoop

Invite your friends over for a game of origami basketball using this great hoop and a scrunched up piece of paper as a ball! You'll need a pencil to draw the net.

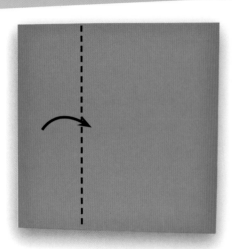

1 Place your paper as shown and make a valley fold a third of the way from the left edge.

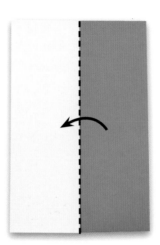

2 Valley fold the right edge over to the left edge.

3 Your paper should look like this.

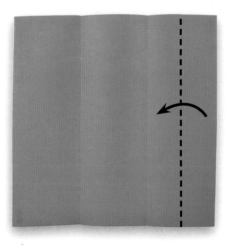

4 Unfold the paper and fold the right edge so it meets the right-hand crease.

5 Fold the left edge so it meets the left-hand crease.

6 Diagonally fold the top right-hand corner down to the left edge.

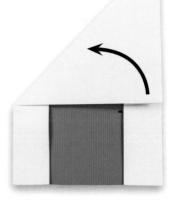

7 Your paper should look like this. Unfold it and then fold the top left-hand corner down to the right edge.

8 Your paper should now look like this. Unfold the fold you made in step 7.

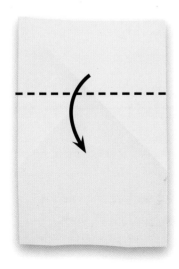

9 Turn the paper over, and fold the top forward, making the crease through the middle of the cross of diagonal creases.

23

Basketball Hoop... continued

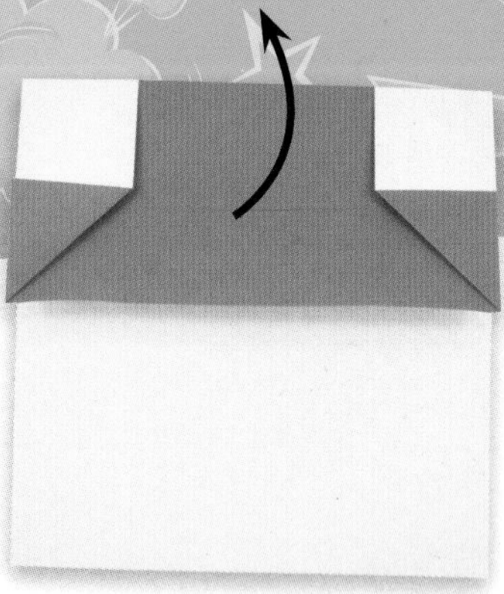

10 Unfold the fold you made in step 9.

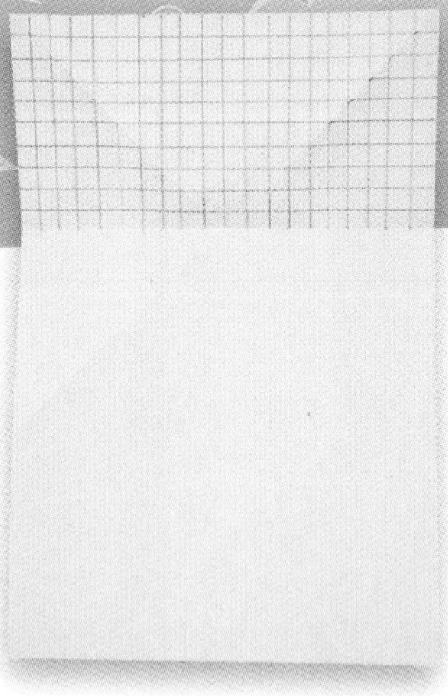

11 Use your pencil to draw a net pattern in the area above the horizontal crease.

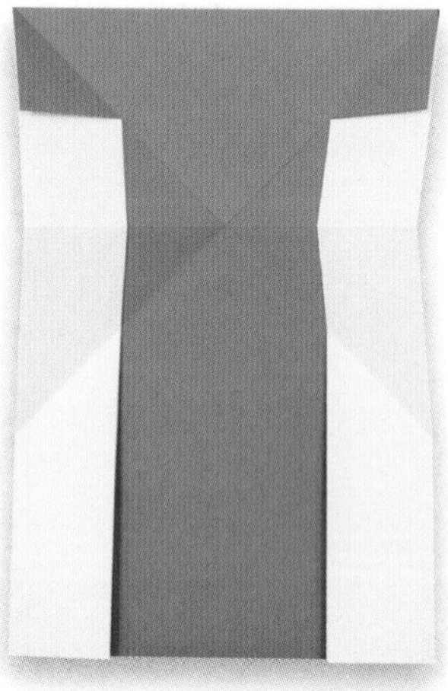

12 Turn the paper over so it looks like this.

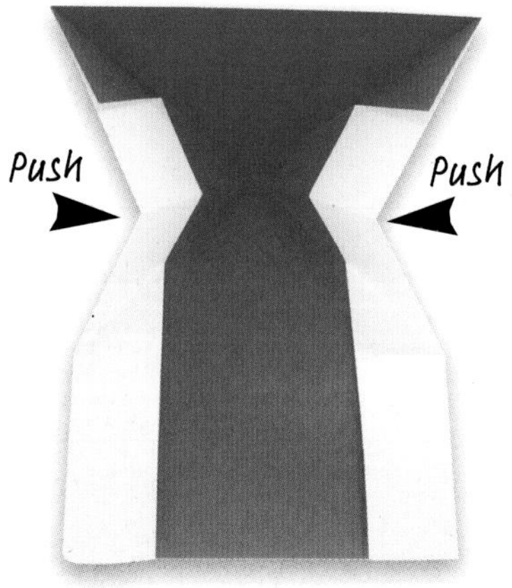

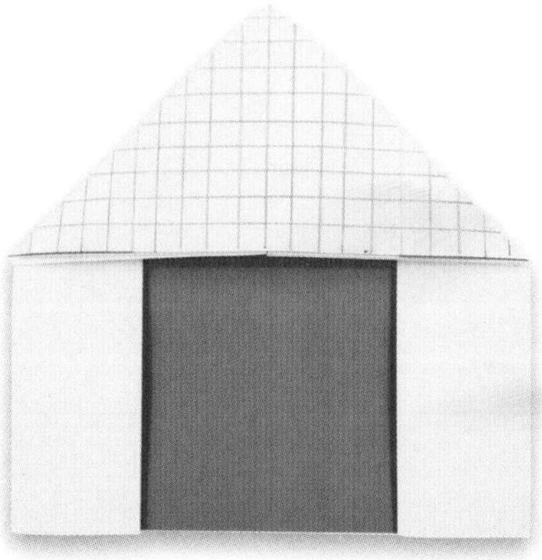

13 Start pushing the two sides of the horizontal crease together, like this.

14 Keep pushing until a triangle shape forms. Flatten it down.

15 Start curling the ends of the triangle toward each other.

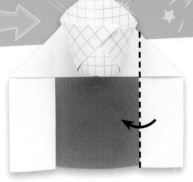

16 Keep curling until the two ends meet, then tuck one end inside the other to hold the basket in place. Fold the right-hand side to the middle.

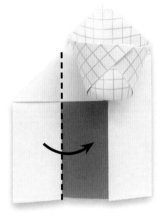

18 Your paper should look like this.

17 Fold the left-hand side to the middle.

19 Open the last two folds up, so the flaps stick out. Now stand your basket up and shoot some hoops!

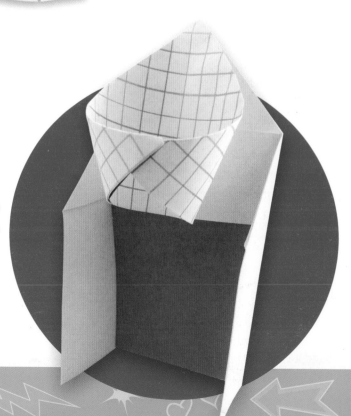

Dice

Dice are used in lots of different games. Follow these instructions to make some dice of your own, draw on the dots with a felt-tip pen, and get rolling!

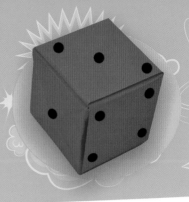

1 You'll need two pieces of paper for this project, which you'll need to fold in exactly the same way.

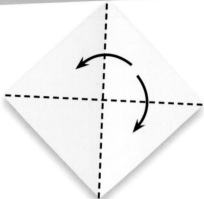

2 Place the first piece of paper like this. Valley fold in half from left to right, and unfold. Then valley fold in half from top to bottom, and unfold.

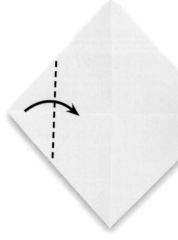

3 Take the left point and fold it over to meet the central line.

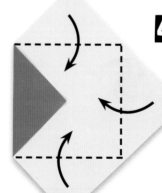

4 Repeat step 3 with the other three points.

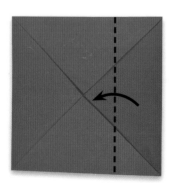

5 Make a vertical valley fold a third of the way from the right side.

6 Fold the left edge all the way over to the right edge to form a tube shape.

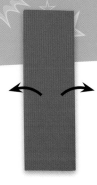

7 Unfold the folds you made in steps 5 and 6.

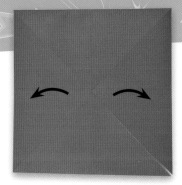

8 Unfold the left and right sides.

9 Your paper should look like this. Make a valley fold a third of the way from the top edge.

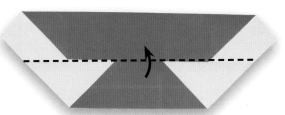

10 Valley fold the bottom edge to the top to make a long thin shape.

11 Take the left point and make a diagonal fold downward at the point of the second crease from the left.

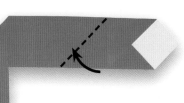

12 Take the right point and make a diagonal fold upward at the point of the second crease from the right.

Dice... continued

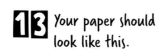

13 Your paper should look like this.

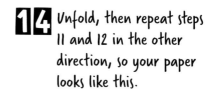

14 Unfold, then repeat steps 11 and 12 in the other direction, so your paper looks like this.

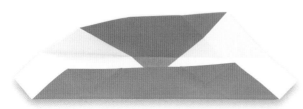

15 Unfold and carefully pull apart the top and bottom flaps so that they're parallel to each other, like this.

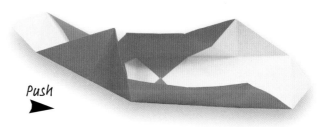

Push

16 Start to gently push the folds on the left-hand side toward you.

17 Turn the paper around so the open side is facing you. Tuck the far side over to form one side of the cube.

Push

18 Now start pushing the folds together on the other side.

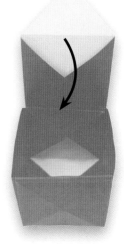

19 Turn the paper around again, and tuck the point over to complete your model.

20 The first half of your dice is now complete.

21 Use the other sheet of paper and repeat steps 1 to 19 to make the other half of the dice.

Push

22 Slightly squeeze the edges of one of the boxes, fit it carefully inside the other box, and push down.

23 Once the two boxes have slotted together, use a felt-tip pen to draw on some dots. Your dice is ready to roll!

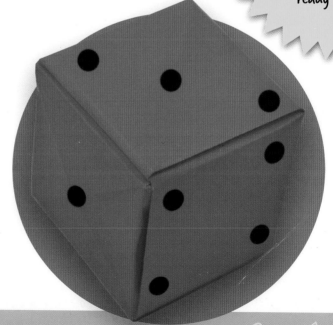

Spinning Top

This terrific top really does spin! It takes a little while to make, but it's guaranteed to provide hours of spinning fun.

MODEL PIECE 1

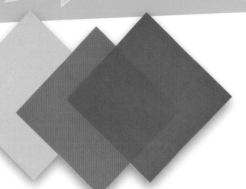

1 To make the spinning top, you need three different sheets of paper. Blue, yellow, and red look good together.

2 Place your first sheet of paper white side up. Valley fold it from top to bottom, then unfold.

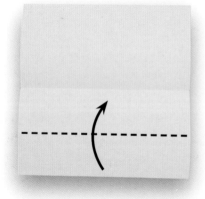

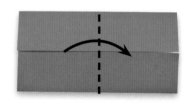

3 Valley fold the bottom edge up to the middle line.

4 Valley fold the top edge to the middle line.

5 Valley fold the paper in half from left to right, then unfold.

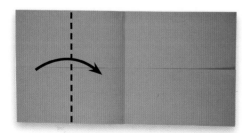

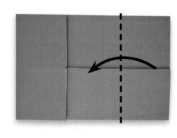

6 Valley fold the left-hand edge to the middle line.

7 Valley fold the right-hand edge to meet the left flap.

8 Your paper should look like this.

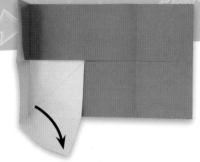

9 Unfold steps 6 and 7.

10 Push up the left-hand edge so it's vertical. Then make a diagonal fold in one of the small squares in the bottom left, like this.

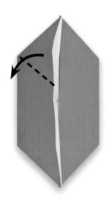

11 Repeat step 10 in the top left, too.

12 Press down the left-hand side to make this shape.

13 Repeat steps 10, 11, and 12 on the right-hand side, so your paper looks like this. Take the top left-hand point and fold it diagonally to the left.

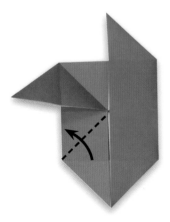

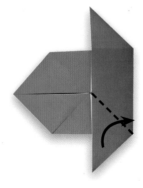

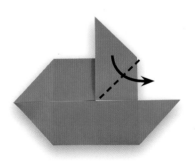

14 Take the bottom left-hand point and fold it diagonally to the left.

15 Take the bottom right-hand point and fold it diagonally to the right.

16 Take the top right-hand point and fold it diagonally to the right.

Spinning Top... continued

17 Your paper should now look like this.

18 Lift up the top left-hand corner and open it out, so it looks like a bird's mouth.

19 Flatten the corner down to form a mini square, like this.

20 Repeat steps 18 and 19 with the three other points. You'll then have four mini squares. In the top left square, valley fold the bottom edge up to meet the central diagonal line.

21 Now fold the top edge of the same square to meet the central diagonal line.

22 Repeat steps 20 and 21 with the other 3 mini squares.

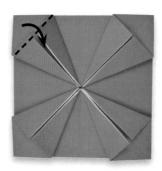

23 Fold over the top left corner of the top left mini square.

24 Repeat step 23 for the other three corners.

25 Your paper should now look like this.

26 In the top left-hand corner, open up the three folds you just made.

27 Lift up the point at the middle so it forms a shape a bit like a bird's mouth.

28 Flatten the paper down, leaving a pointed shape like this.

29 Repeat steps 26, 27, and 28 for the other three corners. Your paper should look like this.

30 On the right-hand side, take the middle point and fold it to the right, like this. Then repeat the step with the other three central points.

31 Fold the top left point in toward the middle.

32 Repeat step 31 with the other 3 corners.

33 Your first model piece is now ready.

Spinning Top... continued

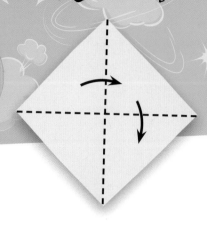

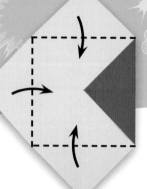

1 With your paper white side up and pointing toward you, make two valley folds, like this. Then unfold.

2 Fold the right-hand corner to the middle point. Then do the same with the other 3 corners.

3 Your paper should look like this.

4 Turn the paper over. Fold the top right-hand corner to the middle point. Do the same with the other three corners.

5 Your paper should look like this.

6 Turn the paper over again, and fold the top right-hand corner to the middle point. Then do the same with the other three corners.

7 Your paper should look like this.

8 Turn the paper over again and fold out the top right flap from the middle point. Do the same with the other three flaps.

9 Your second model piece is now ready. Put it to one side and pick up your third piece of paper.

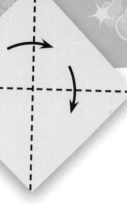

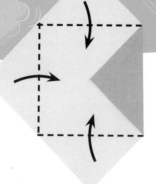

1 Place your paper white side up. Make two valley folds like this, then unfold.

2 Fold the right corner to the middle point. Then do the same with the other three corners.

3 Your paper should look like this. Take the top right corner and fold it to the middle point.

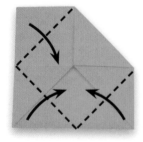

4 Fold the other three corners to the middle.

5 Again, fold the top right-hand corner to the middle.

6 Then fold the other three corners to the middle.

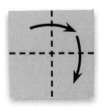

7 Your paper should look like this.

8 Turn the paper over and make two valley folds along the vertical and horizonal lines.

9 Push in the folds made along the vertical and horizontal lines to form a star shape, like this. Now it's time to put it all together!

Spinning Top... continued

PUTTING IT TOGETHER

1 Take Model Piece 2 and insert the top left corner into Model Piece 1, like this.

2 Repeat with the other 3 corners.

3 Now take Model Piece 3 and insert the legs under the flaps of Model Piece 2, like this.

4 All four legs should now be in position and secure.

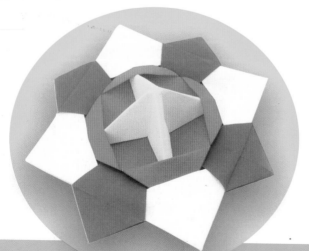

5 Your super spinning top is ready. Let's give it a spin!

Hey Presto!

Amaze your family and astound your friends by folding some magical paper models.

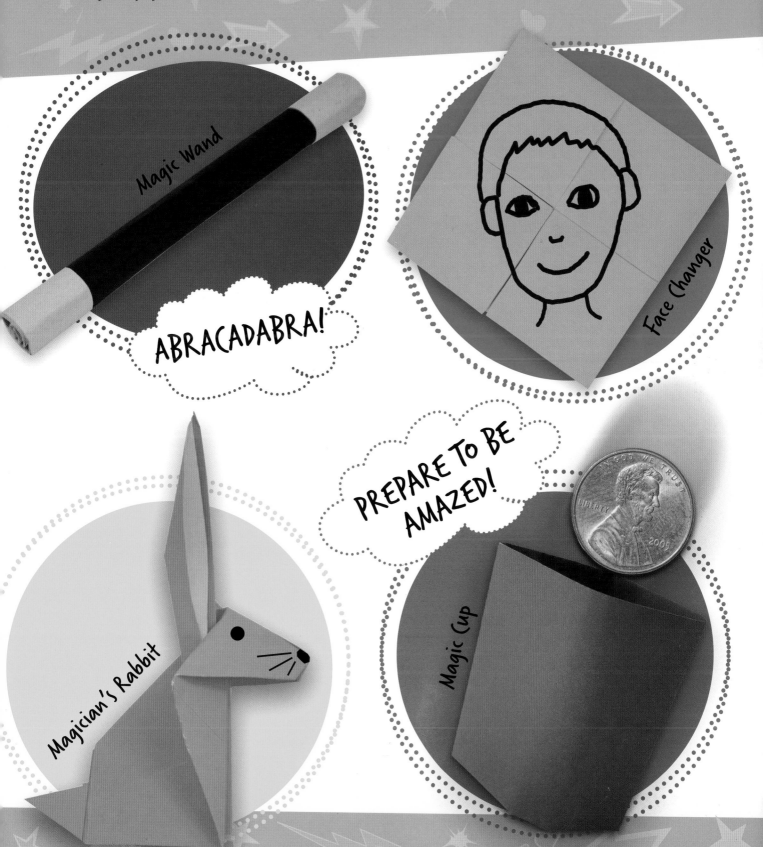

Magic Wand

Face Changer

ABRACADABRA!

PREPARE TO BE AMAZED!

Magician's Rabbit

Magic Cup

Magic Wand

The first thing that all good magicians need is a wand. Follow these simple steps to make your own magic wand and then learn how to perform a trick!

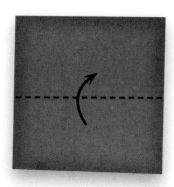

1 Place the paper like this. Valley fold it in half from bottom to top, but don't crease the line.

2 Make two small pinch marks on the left- and right-hand sides. Unfold the paper.

3 Valley fold the bottom edge to the middle, using the pinch marks as a guide, but don't crease the line.

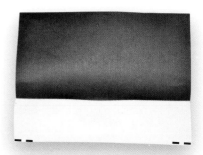

4 Again, just make two small pinch marks, one on the left and one on the right, like this. Unfold.

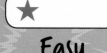

5 Valley fold the bottom edge up to the new pinch marks, but this time make a crease all the way along the line.

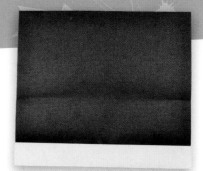

6 Your paper should look like this. Rotate the paper so the white strip is at the top.

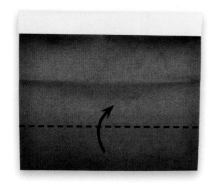

7 Fold the bottom edge up to the pinch marks in the middle. Again, just make two small pinch marks, one on the left and one on the right.

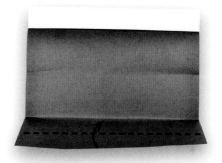

8 Fold the bottom edge up to the pinch marks made in step 7, but this time crease all the way along the line.

9 Rotate the paper 90° so it looks like this. Then turn the paper over.

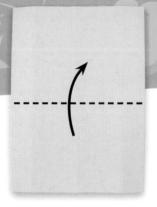

10 Valley fold the paper in half from bottom to top and crease all the way along.

11 Your paper should look like this. Unfold.

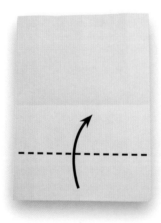

12 Fold the bottom edge to the middle crease and crease all the way along.

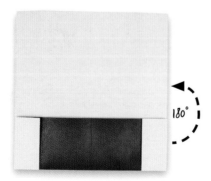

13 Your paper should look like this. Rotate it 180°.

14 Fold the bottom edge up to the top flap.

15 Fold up the bottom edge by about 5 mm (¼ inch).

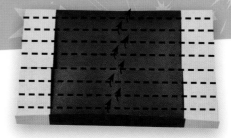

16 Fold over the flap you made in step 15, and then keep repeating this, folding the paper over and over until you get to the top.

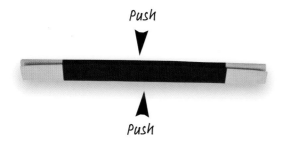

Push

Push

17 You should be left with what looks like a flat wand. Turn it into a round wand by squeezing the sides.

Make Some Magic

If you place your finger inside the flap running down the side of your wand, you can make it look like the wand is magically balancing on your finger, or even floating in mid-air!

18 Your wand is ready for your first trick!

Face Changer

You'll need some pens and pencils to draw the features on your magic face changer. Try to make each face as different as possible!

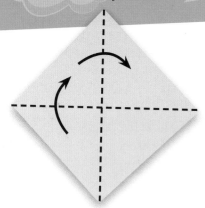

1 With your paper like this, make a diagonal valley fold from left to right and unfold. Then make a diagonal valley fold from top to bottom and unfold.

2 Turn the paper over. Fold the left-hand point to the middle.

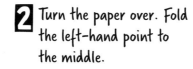

3 Repeat step 2 on the other three sides.

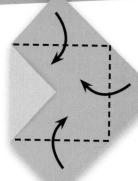

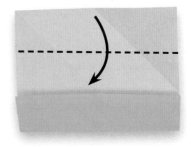

6 Fold the top edge down to the middle.

4 Your paper should look like this. Unfold the folds you made in steps 2 and 3. Then turn it over, so the white side is showing.

5 Turn the paper so a square edge is facing you. Fold the bottom edge up to the middle.

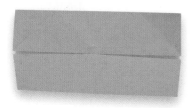

7 Your paper should look like this. Unfold it.

8 Now fold the left edge to the middle.

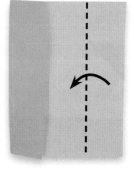

9 Then fold the right edge to the middle.

42

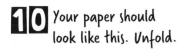

Push

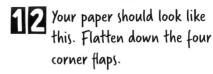

Push ▶   ◀ Push

▲
Push

10 Your paper should look like this. Unfold.

11 Pick the paper up and press it together along its four flat sides, as shown. The paper should begin to fold up.

12 Your paper should look like this. Flatten down the four corner flaps.

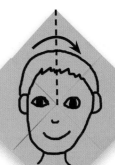

14 Take your pen and draw a face with the hair in the top square, the eyes in the side squares, and the nose and mouth in the bottom square.

15 Flip the top left flap to the right.

13 Rotate the paper so one of the corners is pointing toward you, like this.

16 Draw a new hairstyle for your character, and unfold. Then flip the top right flap to the left and draw a third hairstyle.

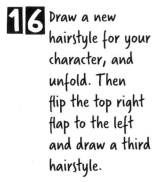

17 Repeat steps 15 and 16 with the other 3 squares, so you have 3 completely different faces. Then have fun changing them around!

Magic Cup

You can use this simple origami cup to perform lots of tricks. Held one way, it's just a normal cup, but turn it around and you've got a special magic cup without a base.

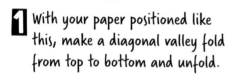

1 With your paper positioned like this, make a diagonal valley fold from top to bottom and unfold.

2 Valley fold the bottom point up to the central line.

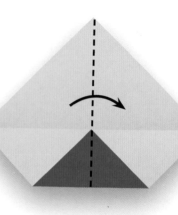

3 Valley fold the paper in half from left to right.

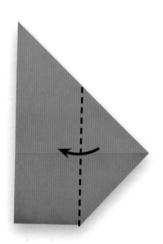

4 Valley fold the right point to the left edge.

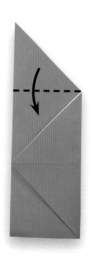

5 Valley fold the top point down to the central line.

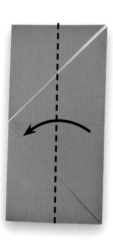

6 Valley fold in half from right to left, then unfold.

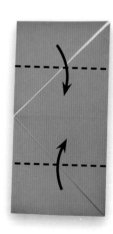

7 Now valley fold the top edge and the bottom edge to the central line, then unfold.

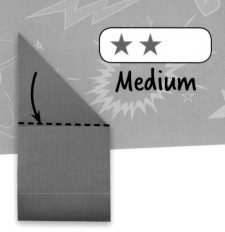

8 Unfold the top left layer.

9 Valley fold the bottom edge up to the top triangle, as shown.

10 Valley fold the top point of the triangle forward and tuck it into the front pocket.

Push

Push   Push

11 Keep tucking until all of the triangle is inside the pocket.

12 Squeeze the sides and it will turn into a cup shape.

13 Your paper should look like this.

Fool Your Friends

Hold the paper shaped like a cup, with your other hand resting underneath it. Get a friend to drop in a coin. Tip it back into their hand to show that the paper is just a cup. Then ask if they have another coin. Turn the cup into a tube while they're searching for one, again with your other hand resting underneath. Get your friend to drop the second coin in. It will fall into your hand. Close your fingers over the coin without your friend seeing and tip the cup back into their hand. When no coin appears, act amazed!

14 From above you can see that it forms a cup. But if you turn it on its side and squeeze, it forms a tube.

Magician's Rabbit

Making a rabbit disappear is one of the great magic tricks. But first you need to make your rabbit. Here's how!

1 Place the paper like this and fold diagonally in half from top to bottom.

2 Diagonally fold the right-hand point down to the bottom point.

3 Diagonally fold the left-hand point down to the bottom point.

4 Diagonally fold the left-hand edge to the central line.

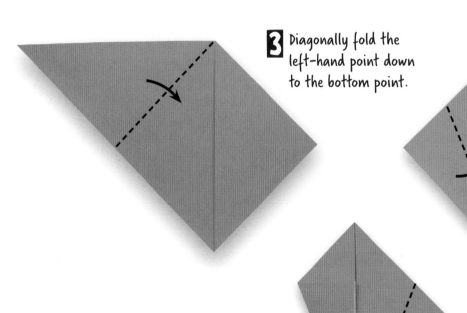

5 Diagonally fold the right-hand edge to the central line.

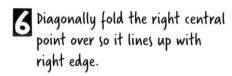

6 Diagonally fold the right central point over so it lines up with right edge.

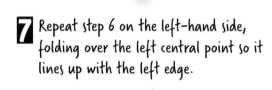

7 Repeat step 6 on the left-hand side, folding over the left central point so it lines up with the left edge.

8 Your paper should look like this.

9 Lift up the fold you made in step 6. Open the fold up so it forms a pocket.

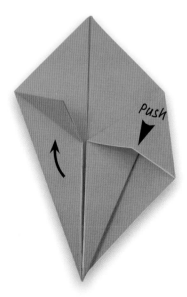

Push

10 Flatten the pocket so it forms a triangle, then repeat step 9 on the other side.

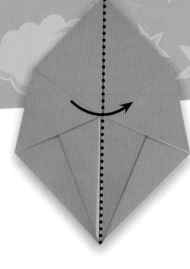

11 Your paper should look like this. Mountain fold it in half from left to right.

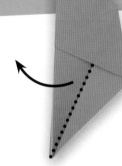

12 Mountain fold the bottom left-hand point up to the left and in-between the other folds.

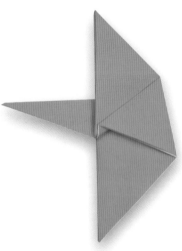

13 Your paper should look like this, with a long point to one side. Turn it over from left to right.

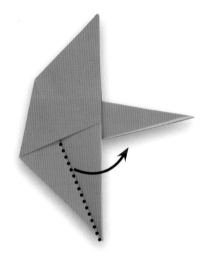

14 Repeat step 12 on the other side; mountain fold the bottom right-hand point up to the right.

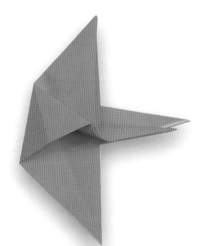

15 Make sure the fold goes inside the other folds, and matches the fold on the other side.

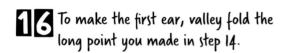

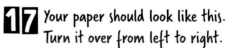

16 To make the first ear, valley fold the long point you made in step 14.

17 Your paper should look like this. Turn it over from left to right.

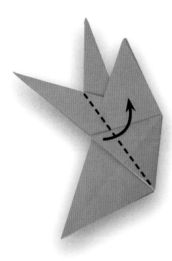

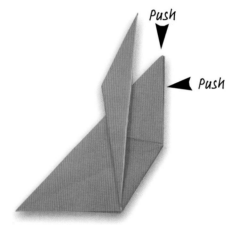

Push

Push

18 To make the second ear, valley fold the long point you made in step 12 to match the other one.

19 Holding the ears at the base, start to make the face by pushing open the top right point and folding it around the ears.

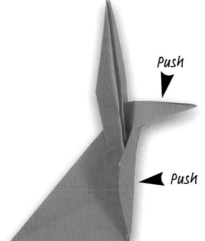

Push

Push

20 Your paper should look like this. Push down the folds to make the face.

Magician's Rabbit... continued

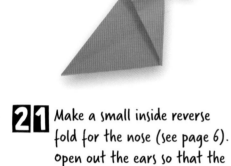

21 Make a small inside reverse fold for the nose (see page 6). Open out the ears so that the white is showing on the inside.

22 To make the tail, make a vertical valley fold like this. Then fold it the other way, so it's also a mountain fold.

23 Make another smaller valley fold near the first fold. Again, fold it the other way, so it's also a mountain fold.

24 Your paper should look like this. Make the two previous folds into an inside reverse fold to make the tail.

25 Draw on eyes and whiskers. Your magic rabbit is ready to perform his first trick!

50

On the Water

Make some waves with this amazing bunch of floating origami models. Try your hand at folding a speedy motorboat or make a paper duckling for the bath!

Duckling

QUACK, QUACK!

Motorboat

Catamaran

Lotus Flower

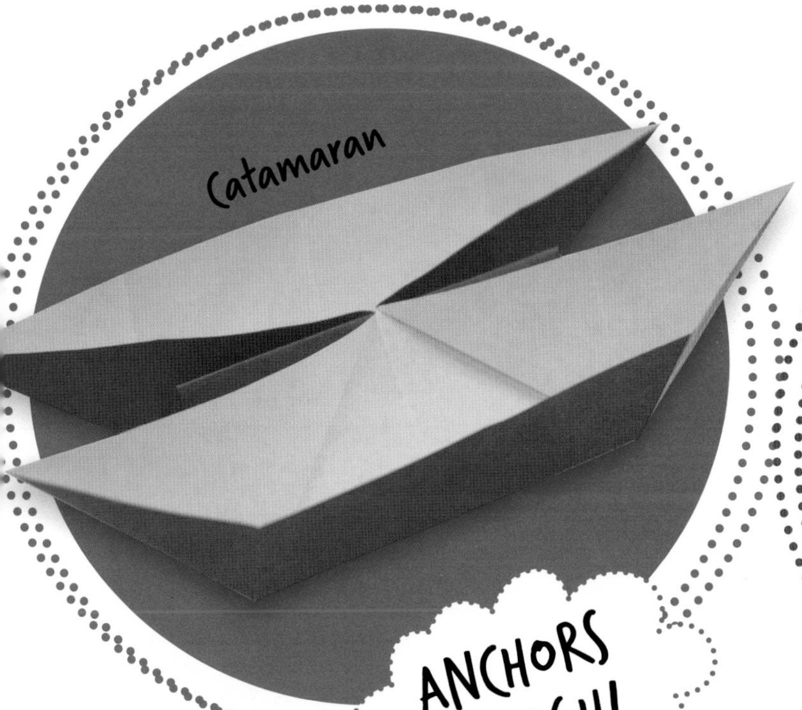

ANCHORS AWEIGH!

Catamaran

A catamaran is a special type of boat with two long, equal-sized hulls. That means this origami catamaran has twice the floating power of a normal boat!

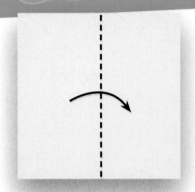

1 Place your paper white side up, like this. Valley fold it in half from left to right.

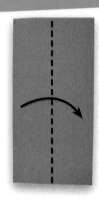

2 Fold the paper in half again from left to right.

3 Your paper should look like this. Unfold and rotate the paper 90° to the left so the fold lines are horizontal.

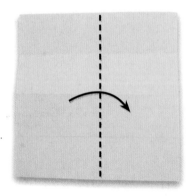

4 Valley fold the paper in half from left to right.

5 Again, valley fold the paper in half from left to right.

6 Your paper should look like this. Unfold it.

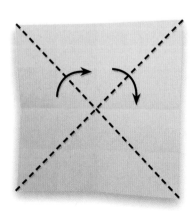

7 Diagonally fold the top left corner to the bottom right, and unfold. Then diagonally fold the top right corner to the bottom left, and unfold.

8 Valley fold the right edge to the middle.

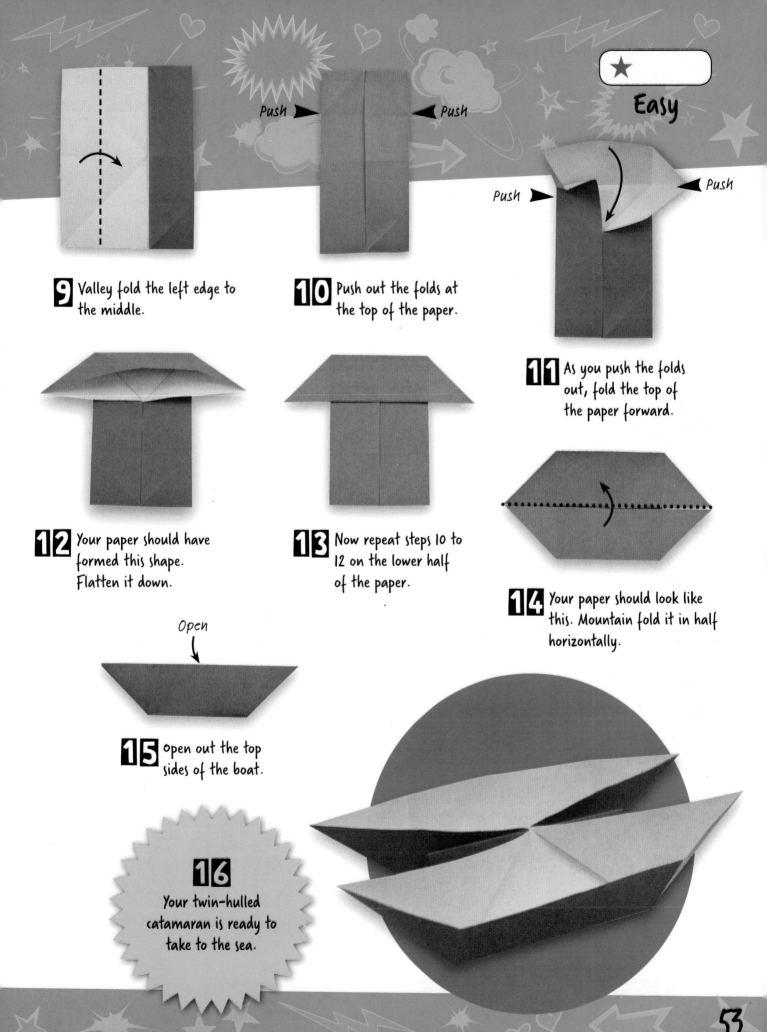

Push ▶   ◀ **Push**

Push ▶   ◀ **Push**

9 Valley fold the left edge to the middle.

10 Push out the folds at the top of the paper.

11 As you push the folds out, fold the top of the paper forward.

12 Your paper should have formed this shape. Flatten it down.

13 Now repeat steps 10 to 12 on the lower half of the paper.

14 Your paper should look like this. Mountain fold it in half horizontally.

Open

15 Open out the top sides of the boat.

16 Your twin-hulled catamaran is ready to take to the sea.

Lotus Flower

The lotus flower grows in water, floating on the surface. This project requires some strong finger power, as you'll need to fold the paper over several times.

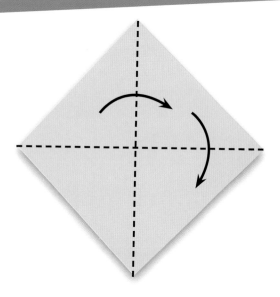

1 Place the paper white side up, with one corner facing you. Make two valley folds as shown, then unfold.

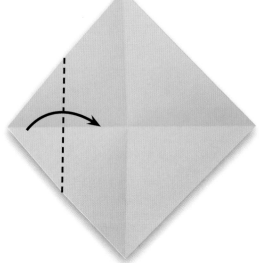

2 Valley fold the left corner to the central line.

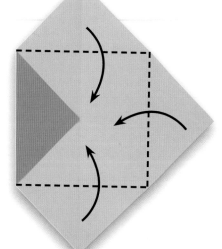

3 Repeat step 2 with the other three corners.

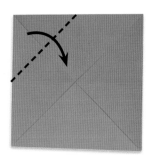

4 Fold the top left corner to the central line.

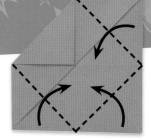

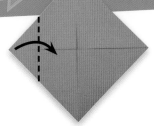

5 Repeat step 4 with the other 3 corners.

6 Again, fold the left corner to the central line.

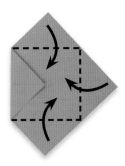

7 Repeat step 6 with the other 3 corners.

8 Your paper should look like this. Turn it over from left to right.

9 For the final time, fold the top left corner to the central point.

10 Repeat step 9 with the other 3 sides.

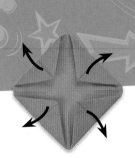

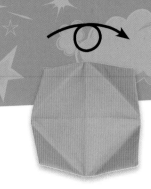

11 Open up the folds you made in steps 9 and 10, so the corners point outward.

12 Your paper should look like this. Turn it over.

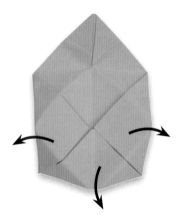

13 Unfold the top point.

14 Repeat step 13 with the other three points.

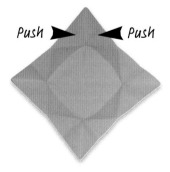

15 Your paper should look like this. Turn it over from right to left.

16 Push the top points together. The other points will begin to come together too.

17 Push the other three points together.

18 Gently open the top point of the model to form a rounded, petal-like shape.

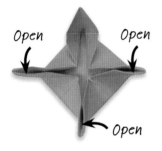

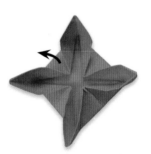

19 Open the other three points to form petal shapes.

20 Your paper should look like this. Carefully reach under the paper and unfold the point beneath the top left edge.

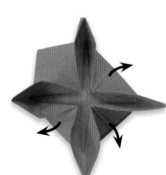

21 Repeat step 20 with the other 3 edges.

22
Plump out your petals and your beautiful lotus is ready to float.

Duckling

Quack, quack! Here comes an origami duckling paddling along the water. Why not make a whole family of ducks and take them all for a swim together?

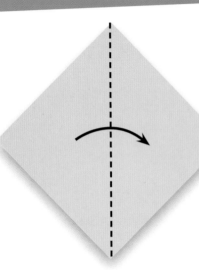

1 Place your paper like this. Make a valley fold from left to right, then unfold.

2 Fold the left corner to the central line.

3 Fold the right corner to the central line.

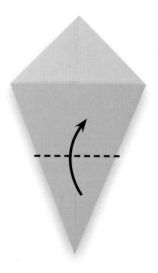

4 Fold the bottom point up to the top.

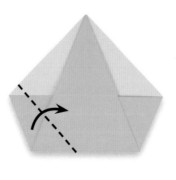

5 Fold the bottom left corner over to the central line.

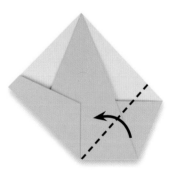

6 Fold the bottom right corner over to the central line.

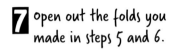

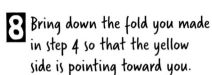

7 Open out the folds you made in steps 5 and 6.

8 Bring down the fold you made in step 4 so that the yellow side is pointing toward you.

9 Your paper should look like this. As you bring the point forward, press its sides together.

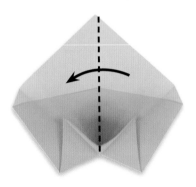

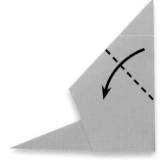

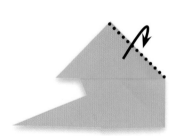

10 When the point is sticking straight at you, valley fold the whole paper in half from right to left.

11 Then make a diagonal valley fold as shown.

12 Now turn the fold you made in step 11 into a mountain fold, to crease the paper really well.

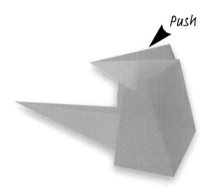

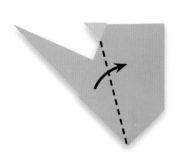

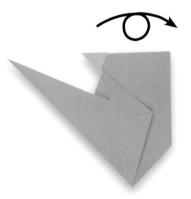

13 Open out the paper and turn the folds you made in steps 11 and 12 into an inside reverse fold (see page 6).

14 Flatten your paper down, so it looks like this. Valley fold the bottom central point, as shown.

15 Your paper should look like this. Turn it over from left to right, and repeat step 14 on the other side.

Duckling... continued

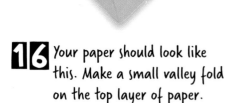

16 Your paper should look like this. Make a small valley fold on the top layer of paper.

17 Now fold the corner you just made the other way, as a mountain fold, and tuck it behind so it's out of sight. Then turn the paper over from left to right, and repeat steps 16 and 17 on the other side.

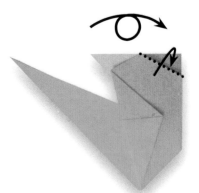

18 Your paper should look like this. Make another small valley fold, as shown.

19 Fold the corner you just made the other way, as a mountain fold, and tuck it behind so it's out of sight. Turn the paper over and repeat steps 18 and 19 on the other side.

20 Your paper should look like this. Fold down the right point, as shown.

21 Fold the point the other way to make a mountain fold. Then flip it over to make an outside reverse fold (see page 6).

22 Your paper should look like this. Flatten it down.

23 Make a valley fold along the top section, as shown.

24 Then make another, smaller valley fold going in the opposite direction.

25 Now turn the folds from steps 23 and 24 into two inside reverse folds, one inside the other (see page 6).

Open

26 Your duckling is almost done. Open up its wings so it can balance on the water.

27
It's time to run the bath. Your duckling is ready for a swim!

Motorboat

The motorboat is the fastest of all boats, zipping across the water at great speeds. Here's how to make a sleek and streamlined origami version.

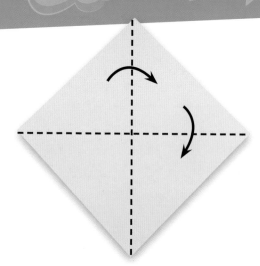

1 Place the paper white side up, with one corner facing you. Make two valley folds as shown, then unfold.

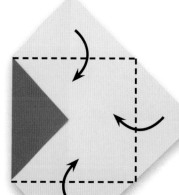

2 Valley fold the left corner to the central line.

3 Repeat step 2 with the other three corners.

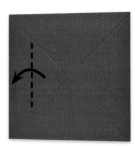

4 Take the central left-hand point and valley fold it back to the left.

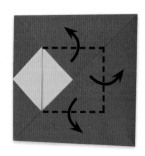

5 Repeat step 4 with the other three central points, as shown.

6 Your paper should now look like this. Unfold the top side.

7 Fold forward the top point, then fold it over again so the point is hidden.

8 Repeat steps 6 and 7 on the bottom side.

9 Mountain fold the top and bottom section back, as shown.

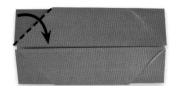

10 Your paper should look like this. Turn it over from left to right.

11 Fold the top left corner down to the central line.

12 Repeat step 11 with the other 3 corners.

13 Fold the top right corner down to meet the central line. Do the same with the other three corners.

14 Fold the top point down to the middle.

15 Fold the bottom point up to the middle.

63

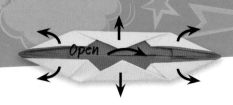

16 Unfold the folds made in steps 13 to 15 and start to open up the central horizontal folds.

17 Your paper should look like this. Keep opening up the central folds.

18 When the folds are wide apart, like this, push the model up from below to turn the boat inside out, so the red side bulges outward.

19 Your paper should look like this. Turn it over.

20 Lift up the white fold of paper on the left side.

21 Now lift up the white fold of paper on the right side.

22 Your motorboat is ready to race!

Action Packed

From inflatable fish to hens that lay paper eggs, this chapter is full of great models that really move!

Inflatable Fish

Beating Hearts

IT MUST BE LOVE!

Egg-Laying Hen

Jumping Horse

CLUCK, CLUCK!

Inflatable Fish

Follow these instructions to make your very own origami goldfish. This one also comes with a special surprise... it expands when you blow into it!

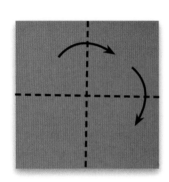

1 Place your paper like this. Valley fold in half from top to bottom, and unfold. Then valley fold in half from left to right, and unfold.

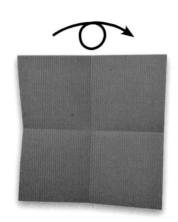

2 Turn your paper over.

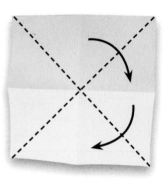

3 Valley fold your paper diagonally both ways, like this, and unfold.

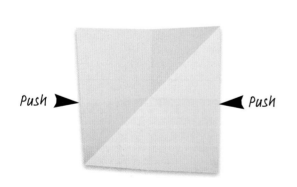

Push ► ◄ Push

4 Push the left and right edges of your paper in toward each other.

5 The paper should start to fold in on itself.

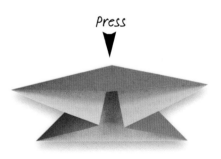

Press ▼

6 Keep pushing so the paper forms a triangle. Press it flat.

7 On the top layer, valley fold the bottom right corner up to the top.

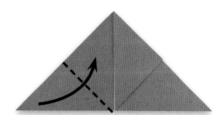

8 Repeat step 7 on the left-hand side, to form a diamond shape.

9 On the top layer, fold the right point of the diamond over to the central line.

10 Repeat step 9 on the left-hand side.

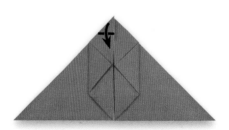

11 On the top layer, fold the top right point down to meet the fold made in step 9.

12 Repeat step 11 on the left-hand side.

Inflatable Fish... continued

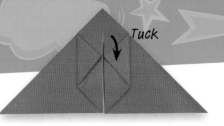

Tuck

13 Tuck the fold you made in step 11 into the fold you made in step 9.

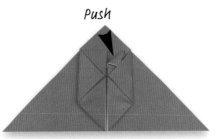

Push

14 Keep pushing until the fold is all the way in.

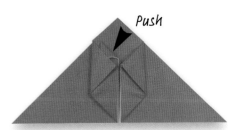

Push

15 Repeat steps 13 and 14 on the left-hand side.

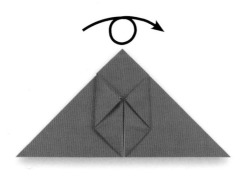

16 Your paper should look like this. Turn it over from left to right.

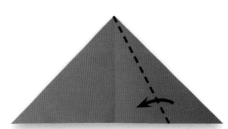

17 Fold the right point over to meet the central line.

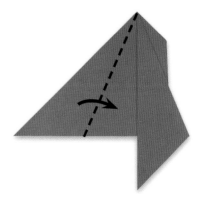

18 Repeat step 17 on the left-hand side.

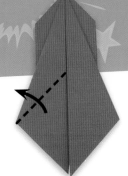

19 Valley fold the bottom left point over to the left, as shown.

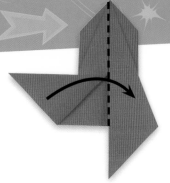

20 Fold the entire left-hand flap over to the right.

21 Flatten the paper down.

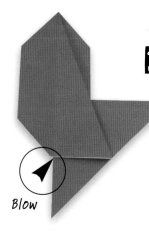

22 To inflate your goldfish, carefully blow into the area circled here.

Blow

23 Your goldfish is ready. Why not make him a few more fishy friends to play with?

Beating Heart

This is a romantic origami heart with a difference...
it really beats! With a bit of skill, you should be able to
make it beat really fast.

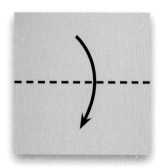

1 Place your paper white side up with a
straight edge facing you. Valley fold it in
half from top to bottom, then unfold.

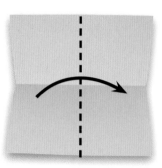

2 Valley fold the paper in half
from left to right.

3 Valley fold the top
left corner down to
the central line.

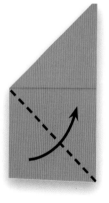

4 Now fold the bottom
left corner up to the
central line.

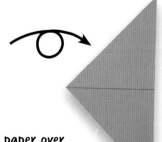

5 Turn the paper over
from left to right.

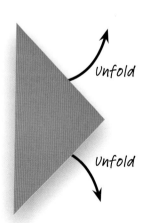

Unfold

Unfold

6 Unfold the folds you
made in steps 3 and 4.

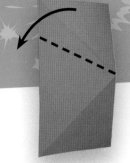

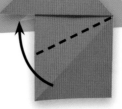

7 Make a diagonal valley fold in the top half, like this, and unfold. Then bring the top left point down and to the left, to make the shape shown in step 8.

8 Repeat on the bottom half, making a diagonal fold and then bringing the bottom left point up to the left.

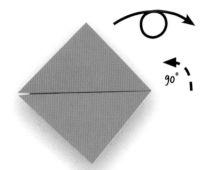

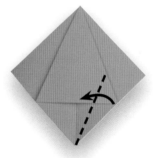

90°

9 Your paper should look like this. Turn it 90° to the left, then turn it over from left to right.

10 Your paper should look like this. Make a small diagonal valley fold on the right side, as shown.

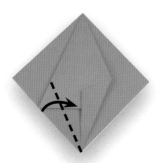

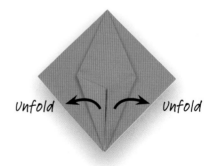

Unfold   Unfold

11 Make a small diagonal valley fold on the left-hand side, as shown.

12 Open up the folds you made in steps 10 and 11.

Beating Heart... continued

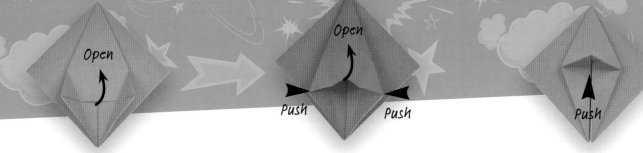

13 Start opening up the horizontal flap, as shown.

14 As you open the horizontal flap, start pushing the two edges on either side together.

15 As the two sides come together, they'll form a triangular shape at the top. Push this up and flatten it down.

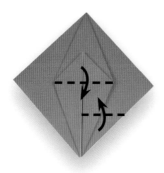

16 Your paper should look like this. Valley fold the central point forward so it's standing upright. This will be the handle. Then valley fold the bottom right point to the middle.

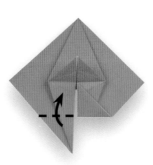

17 Valley fold the bottom left point to the middle too.

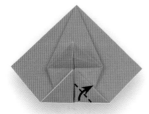

18 Diagonally valley fold the bottom right point to meet the edge of the fold you made in step 16, as shown.

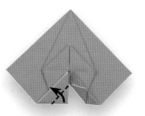

19 Diagonally valley fold the bottom left point to meet the edge of the fold you made in step 17, like this.

20 Your paper should look like this. Rotate it 180°.

21 Take the top right flap and start to tuck it behind the central folds of the paper.

22 Keep tucking until most of the flap is out of sight.

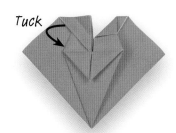

Tuck

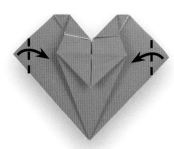

23 Now repeat steps 21 and 22 on the left-hand side.

24 Your paper should look like this. Make small, equal-sized valley folds on the left- and right-hand sides.

26 Hold the handle between your thumb and first two fingers and push them forward to make the heart beat.

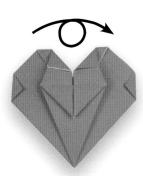

25 Turn the paper over and your heart is ready.

Jumping Horse

This origami horse will perform forward somersaults right before your very eyes. You'll need scissors to complete your model, so ask an adult to help you.

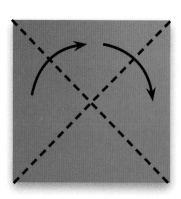

1 Place your paper as shown. Valley fold the paper in half diagonally both ways, then unfold.

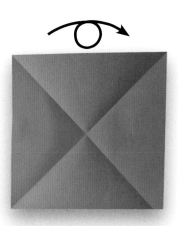

2 Your paper should look like this. Turn it over.

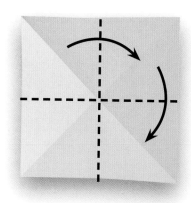

3 Valley fold the paper in half from top to bottom, and unfold. Then valley fold it in half from left to right, and unfold.

Push   Push

4 Rotate the paper, so that a corner is facing you. Then bring the two outer corners in toward each other.

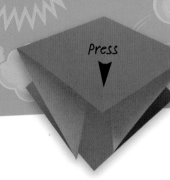

Press

5 As you push, the paper should start folding up into a small square, like this. Flatten it down.

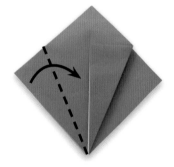

6 Valley fold the right corner of the top layer over to the central line.

7 Valley fold the left corner of the top layer over to the central line.

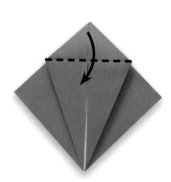

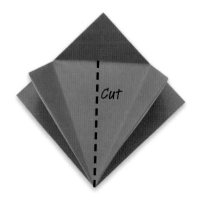

Cut

8 Valley fold the top point down, as shown.

9 Open up the folds you made in steps 6, 7, and 8.

10 Use scissors to make a straight cut, in the top layer only, from the bottom point to the top horizontal fold.

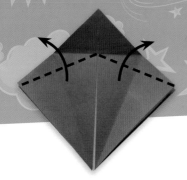

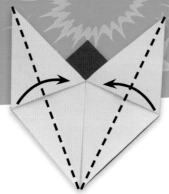

11 Your paper should look like this. Valley fold the top layer up on both the left and right sides.

12 Your paper should look like this. Valley fold the left side of the top layer over to the central line. Then do the same on the right-hand side.

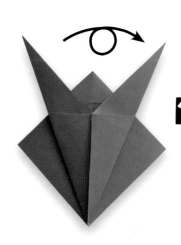

13 Your paper should look like this. Turn it over from left to right, and then repeat steps 6 to 12 on the other side.

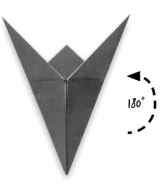

14 Your paper should look like this. Rotate it 180°.

15 Valley fold the top right point over to the right, as shown.

16 Now fold it the other way, so it's also a mountain fold. Then turn it into an inside reverse fold (see page 6). This is your horse's tail.

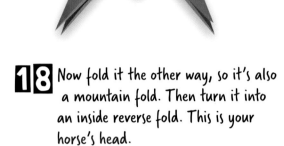

17 Make a valley fold near the tip of the top left point.

18 Now fold it the other way, so it's also a mountain fold. Then turn it into an inside reverse fold. This is your horse's head.

19 Start forming a nose by making a small valley fold at the end of the head.

20 Fold it the other way, so it's also a mountain fold. Then turn it into another inside reverse fold. Your horse is ready to perform!

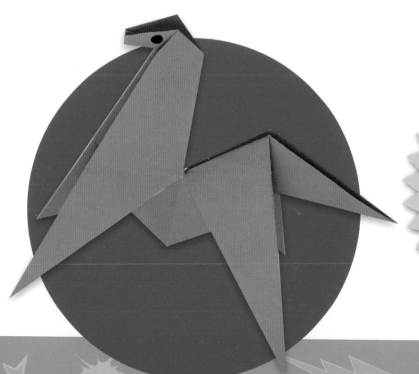

21

To make him jump, flick his tail hard up in the air and he should perform a forward somersault... and land on his feet!

Egg-Laying Hen

With just a single piece of paper you can make both a hen and a little egg. You'll need some scissors for the final stage, so ask an adult to help you.

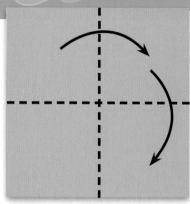

1 Place your paper like this. Valley fold in half from top to bottom, and unfold. Then valley fold in half from left to right, and unfold.

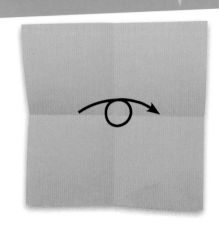

2 Turn your paper over.

3 Diagonally valley fold the top left corner to the bottom right, and unfold.

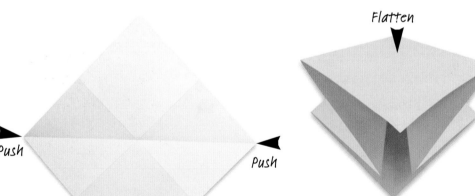

Push

Push

4 Turn your paper so the diagonal fold you made in step 3 is now horizontal and a corner is facing you. Start pushing the left- and right-hand sides together.

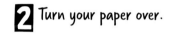

Flatten

5 As you push, the paper should start to fold up into a small square, like this. Flatten it down.

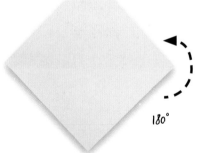

180°

6 Your paper should look like this. Rotate it 180°, so the open end is at the top.

78

7 Valley fold the top point of the top layer down to the bottom.

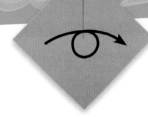

8 Your paper should look like this. Turn it over from left to right.

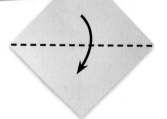

9 Again, valley fold the top point of the top layer down to the bottom.

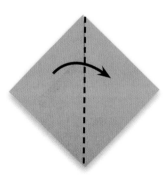

10 Valley fold the left corner of the top layer all the way over to the right.

11 Your paper should look like this. Turn it over, and repeat step 10 on the other side.

12 Then valley fold the left corner of the top layer to the central line.

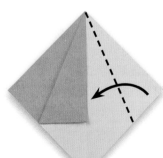

13 Now do the same on the right-hand side.

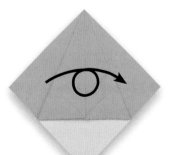

14 Your paper should look like this. Turn it over from left to right.

15 Valley fold the right corner to the central line.

16 Valley fold the left corner to the central line, too.

17 Your paper should look like this.

18 Fold the left flap all the way over to the right.

19 Turn the paper over from left to right, then again fold the left flap all the way to the right.

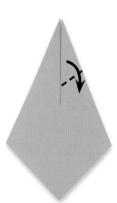

20 Your paper should look like this with a clear gap between the top two points. To start making the tail, make a diagonal valley fold on the top right point, as shown.

21 Now fold the top right point back the other way, so it's also a mountain fold. Then turn it into an inside reverse fold (see page 6).

22 Open the right side up a little. Then mountain fold the tip of the tail downward, and tuck it underneath.

23 Your paper should look like this. Flatten it down.

24 Start to make the head by valley folding the left point over to the left, as shown.

25 Now fold the point the other way, so it's also a mountain fold, then turn it into an inside reverse fold.

26 Your paper should look like this. Make a second, smaller inside reverse fold going the other way, to finish the head.

27 Make a third inside reverse fold going back the other way to form the beak.

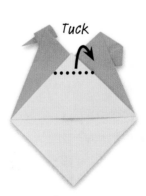

Tuck

28 Your paper should look like this. Valley fold the bottom point of the top layer up, as shown.

29 Tuck the point behind the middle flap.

Cut

30 Take your scissors and make a horizontal cut through the paper about 2 cm (3/4 inches) from the bottom.

31 You'll be left with two pieces of paper, like this.

32 Take the smaller piece of paper and mountain fold the right point of the top layer behind.

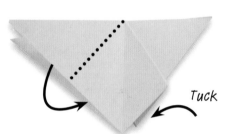

Tuck

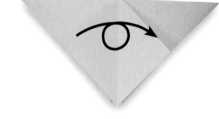

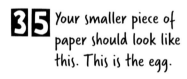

33 Tuck the flap behind. Then repeat on the left-hand side.

34 Your paper should look like this. Turn it over from left to right and repeat steps 32 and 33 on the other side.

35 Your smaller piece of paper should look like this. This is the egg.

36
Slide the egg into the top of your chicken. Move the side flaps up and down and watch the egg pop out of the bottom. It looks like your hen has laid her first egg!

Snap, Snap!

This chapter will show you how to fold a fabulous bunch of snapping origami characters, from barking dogs to kissing frogs!

WOOF, WOOF!

Barking Dog

Pecking Chicken

MAYBE I'LL TURN INTO A PRINCE!

Kissing Frog

Gulping Fish

Gulping Fish

It only takes a few minutes of careful paper folding to create this hungry origami fish with its great, gulping mouth.

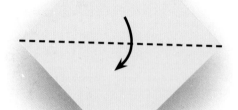

1 Place your paper white side up, with a corner facing you. Valley fold it in half from top to bottom, then unfold.

2 Valley fold the bottom corner up to the central line.

3 Valley fold the top corner down to the central line.

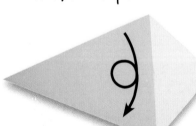

4 Your paper should look like this. Turn it over from top to bottom.

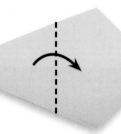

5 Valley fold the paper in half from left to right.

6 Your paper should look like this. Turn it over from top to bottom.

7 Fold the top corner down to the central line.

8 Fold the bottom corner up to the central line.

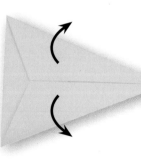

9 Your paper should look like this. Unfold the folds you made in steps 7 and 8, but leave the corners sticking up in the air.

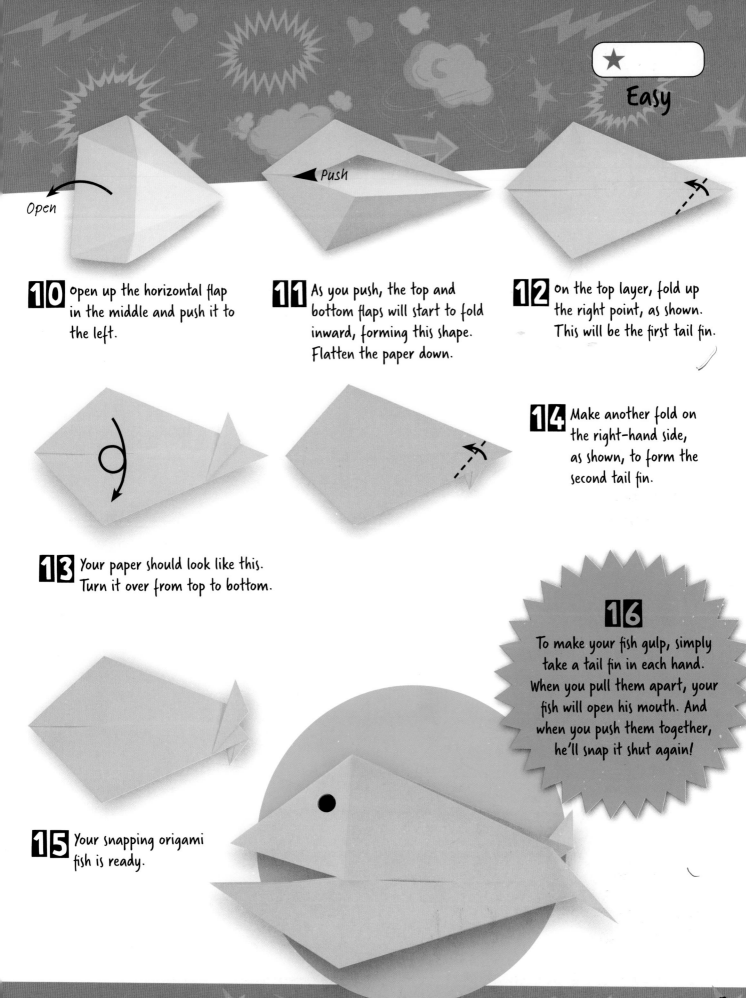

10 Open up the horizontal flap in the middle and push it to the left.

Open

11 As you push, the top and bottom flaps will start to fold inward, forming this shape. Flatten the paper down.

Push

12 On the top layer, fold up the right point, as shown. This will be the first tail fin.

13 Your paper should look like this. Turn it over from top to bottom.

14 Make another fold on the right-hand side, as shown, to form the second tail fin.

15 Your snapping origami fish is ready.

16 To make your fish gulp, simply take a tail fin in each hand. When you pull them apart, your fish will open his mouth. And when you push them together, he'll snap it shut again!

Pecking Chicken

Follow these simple instructions to make a paper chicken that pecks at the ground, just like a real bird hunting for tasty things to eat.

1 Place your paper like this. Valley fold it in half from right to left, then unfold.

2 Valley fold the right-hand point to the middle.

3 Valley fold the left-hand point to the middle.

4 Your paper should look like this. Turn it over from left to right.

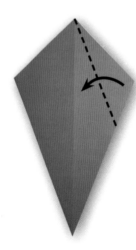

5 Fold the right point to the central line.

6 Fold the left point to the central line.

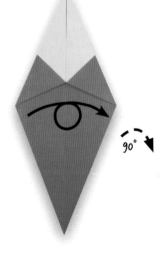

7 Flip the paper over from left to right. Then rotate it 90° to the right.

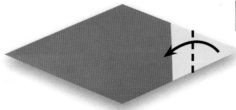

8 Your paper should look like this. Fold the right-hand point to the left, as shown.

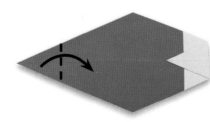

9 Then fold the left-hand point to the right, like this.

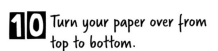

10 Turn your paper over from top to bottom.

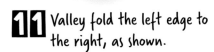

11 Valley fold the left edge to the right, as shown.

12 Then mountain fold the paper in half.

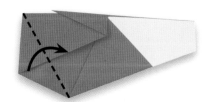

13 Make a diagonal valley fold, as shown.

14 Now fold it the other way so it's also a mountain fold.

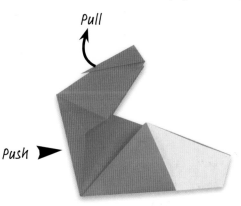

Pull

Push ▶

15 Push the folds you made in steps 13 and 14 to the right and pull up to make the neck. Then pull the head up and crease the beak in position.

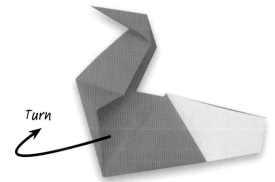

Turn

16 Your chicken is almost ready to get pecking! Turn it around, so the head is facing away from you.

Insert thumb   Insert thumb

17 Insert your thumbs into the two wing pockets, as shown.

18 Push your thumbs to the side and the chicken will lower its head to peck. Put your thumbs back together and it will raise its head again.

Push

Push

Barking Dog

Woof, woof! This barking dog is very cute. Once you've mastered the folds, why not make him a few friends to play with?

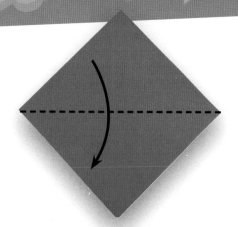

1 Place your paper as shown. Valley fold it in half from top to bottom.

2 Diagonally fold the bottom corner of the top layer up to meet the top edge.

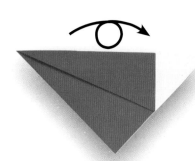

3 Turn the paper over from left to right.

4 Again, diagonally fold the bottom corner of the top layer up to the top edge, so it matches the other side.

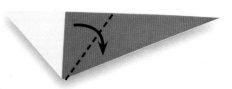

5 Valley fold the left corner of the top layer down to the bottom, as shown.

6 Turn the paper over from left to right and repeat step 5 on the other side.

7 Your paper should look like this. Again, turn it over from left to right.

8 Using the fold you made in step 5 as a guide, fold the left-hand point down to the bottom, as shown.

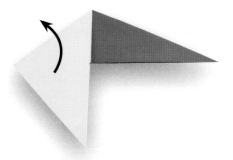

9 Unfold the fold you made in step 8.

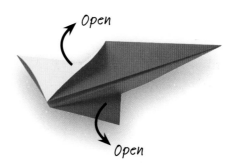

Open

Open

10 Start to open out the red side of the paper.

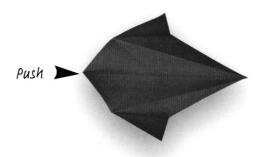

Push

11 Your paper should look like this. Push the left point to the right to form an inside reverse fold (see page 6).

90°

Unfold

12 Unfold the two small triangular flaps, front and back. Rotate the paper 90° to the left. Then turn over from left to right.

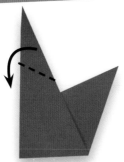

13 Make a valley fold in the left point, as shown.

14 Fold it back the other way so it's also a mountain fold.

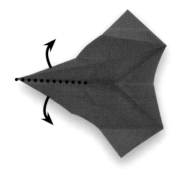

15 Open up the left-hand point and start folding it the other way, as a mountain fold. Bring the sides down to create an outside reverse fold (see page 6).

16 Your paper should look like this. Flatten it down.

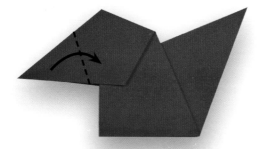

17 Start making the head by valley folding the left point back to the right, as shown. Fold it the other way so it's also a mountain fold.

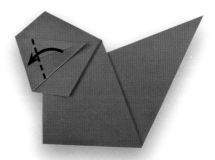

18 Make another valley fold going back to the left. Again, fold it the other way, so it's also a mountain fold.

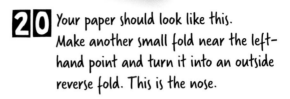

19 Now turn the folds you made in steps 17 and 18 into two inside reverse folds (see page 6), one inside the other.

20 Your paper should look like this. Make another small fold near the left-hand point and turn it into an outside reverse fold. This is the nose.

21 Make the tail by valley folding the right point back to the left, as shown. Fold it the other way so it's also a mountain fold.

22 Make another valley fold, slightly further to the right, as shown. Again, fold it the other way so it's also a mountain fold.

24 Your dog is ready! To make him bark, simply hold his front feet and pull his tail. His head will nod up and down (you'll have to add the sound effects).

23 Now turn the folds you made in steps 21 and 22 into two inside reverse folds, one inside the other.

Pull

Hold here

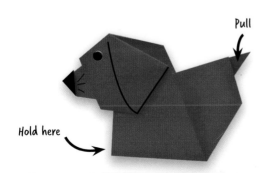

Kissing Frog

In most fairy tales, the combination of a frog and a kiss usually results in a handsome prince appearing. Here, it'll just provide plenty of origami fun.

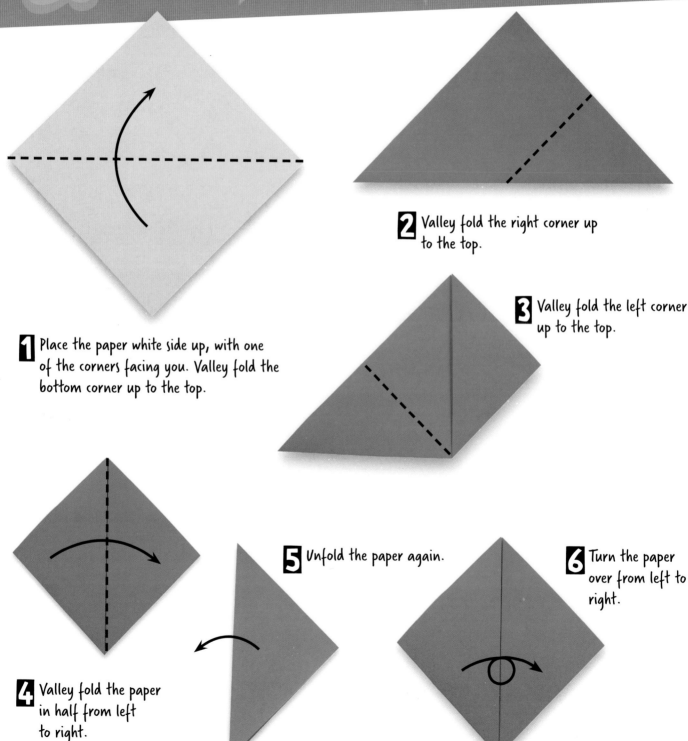

1 Place the paper white side up, with one of the corners facing you. Valley fold the bottom corner up to the top.

2 Valley fold the right corner up to the top.

3 Valley fold the left corner up to the top.

4 Valley fold the paper in half from left to right.

5 Unfold the paper again.

6 Turn the paper over from left to right.

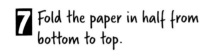

7 Fold the paper in half from bottom to top.

8 Unfold the paper again.

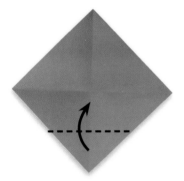

9 Fold the bottom point up to the central line.

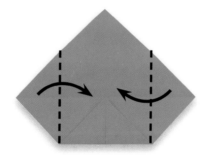

10 Now repeat step 9 on the left and right sides.

11 Fold the top right point down to meet the middle point, as shown.

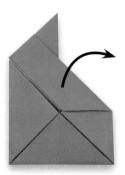

12 Your paper should look like this. Unfold the last fold.

13 Repeat step 11 on the left side.

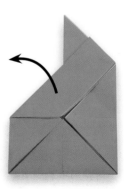

14 Unfold the last fold.

Kissing Frog... continued

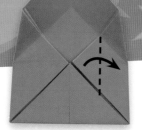

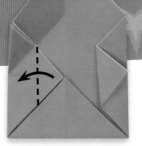

15 Fold the right middle point over to the right-hand side.

16 Then fold the left middle point to the left-hand side.

17 Your paper should look like this. Turn it over from left to right.

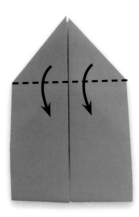

18 On the top layer, fold down the top two points.

19 Fold the central right point up to the right-hand edge.

20 Take the same point and fold it back to the central line.

21 Take the same point again and fold it down to the bottom point of the triangle.

22 Open up the two pieces of paper in the fold you made in step 21.

23 Your paper should look like this. Press it down.

24 Fold the top layer up to make the first eye.

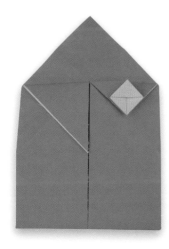

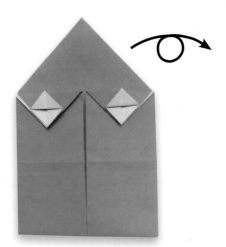

25 Now repeat steps 19 to 24 on the left-hand side to make the second eye.

26 Your paper should look like this. Turn it over from left to right.

27 Make a diagonal valley fold in the bottom triangle starting from the right-hand corner, as shown.

28 Unfold the fold you made in step 27 and then make the same fold on the left-hand side.

Kissing Frog... continued

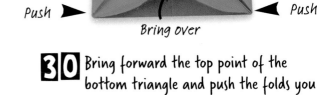

Push ▶   ◀ Push

Bring over

29 Your paper should look like this. Unfold the fold you made in step 28.

30 Bring forward the top point of the bottom triangle and push the folds you made in steps 27 and 28 toward each other to form the feet.

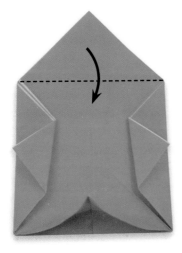

32 Bring the top of the mouth down and curve it slightly so it's pointing downward. Fold up the eyes.

31 To make the mouth, fold down the top point of the top layer, but don't crease. Curve it slightly so it's pointing upward. This is the bottom half of the mouth.

33 To get your frog prince to pucker up, simply press his sides together.

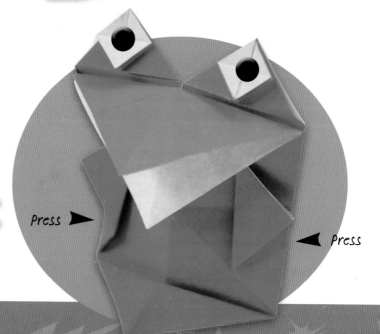

Press ▶   ◀ Press